D1710906

Sea Urchins

A Buddy Book by
Deborah Coldiron

ABDO
Publishing Company

UNDERWATER
WORLD

VISIT US AT

www.abdopublishing.com

Published by ABDO Publishing Company, 8000 West 78th Street, Edina, Minnesota 55439.

Printed in the United States.

Coordinating Series Editor: Sarah Tieck
Contributing Editor: Michael P. Goecke
Graphic Design: Deborah Coldiron
Cover Photograph: Photos.com
Interior Photographs/Illustrations: Brandon Cole Marine Photography (pages 15, 19, 25); Clipart.com (page 17); Corel (page 9); ImageMix (page 29); iStockphoto.com: Stephanie Grimes (page 23); PeterArnold.com: Jonathan Bird/Peter Arnold Inc. (page 27), Wolfgang Poelzer (page 22); Photos.com (pages 7, 11, 21, 22, 23, 28, 30)

Library of Congress Cataloging-in-Publication Data

Coldiron, Deborah.
  Sea urchins / Deborah Coldiron.
    p. cm.-- (Underwater world)
  Includes index.
  ISBN 978-1-60453-137-4
  1. Sea urchins--Juvenile literature. I. Title.

  QL384.E2C64 2009
  593.9'5 -- dc22

                                                2008005051

Table Of Contents

The World Of Sea Urchins

Every living creature needs water. Some animals not only need water, they live in it, too.

Scientists have found more than 250,000 kinds of plants and animals living underwater. And, they believe there could be one million more! The sea urchin is one animal that makes its home in this underwater world.

Water covers 70 percent of Earth's surface.

Sea urchins are bottom dwellers. These spiky creatures are covered in spines.

The smallest sea urchins are less than one-half inch (1 cm) across. Larger sea urchins reach nearly 12 inches (30 cm) in length!

There are about 700 sea urchin **species** in our underwater world. Scientists find these bottom dwellers in shallow and deep ocean waters. But, most sea urchins prefer rocky seafloors in shallow areas.

Often, sea urchins of the same species live near one another.

A Closer Look

Underneath a sea urchin's spines is a ball-shaped skeleton called a test.

The red sea urchin is one of the largest known sea urchins. Its test is about seven inches (18 cm) wide. Each of its spines is about three inches (8 cm) long.

FAST FACTS

Many red sea urchins are not red at all. Most often, they are dark purple.

Sea urchin tests sometimes
wash up on the seashore.
Many people collect them
for their variety and beauty.

Instead of a front and a back, a sea urchin has a top and a bottom. The sea urchin's mouth is located in the center of its bottom side. It contains five teeth.

FAST FACTS

Sea urchins belong to a group of animals known as echinoderms. *Echinoderm* means "spiny-skinned."

The Body Of A Sea Urchin

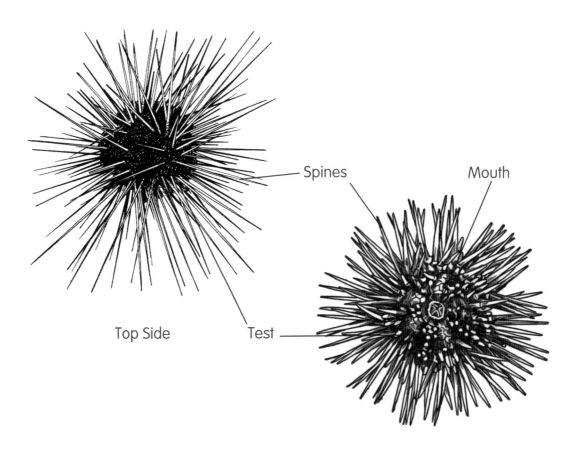

Top Side

Spines

Test

Mouth

Bottom Side

On The Move

Hundreds of tiny tube feet cover a sea urchin's bottom side. These feet work together to help the sea urchin walk.

Pencil urchins have very thick spines. These and other sea urchins can use their spines to move about.

A sea urchin has a madreporite (MA-druh-pawr-ite) on its top side. This opening is located near the center of its test.

Seawater enters the madreporite. Then, it moves throughout the sea urchin's body. The water gives its tube feet the **suction** they need to grip and move.

Madreporite

The madreporite helps the
sea urchin take in water.

A Growing Sea Urchin

A sea urchin begins life as a tiny egg. Females release their eggs into the water. At the same time, males attempt to **fertilize** the eggs. If fertilized, the eggs may hatch and become larvae (LAHR-vee).

FAST FACTS A single female sea urchin may release millions of eggs at one time!

Sea urchin eggs look like clouds in the water.

For a while, the larvae drift along with **plankton**. As they grow, the larvae change shape and sink to the seafloor. Sea urchins take two to five years to become adults.

Some people think a sea urchin larva *(above)* looks a bit like an artist's easel *(right)*.

Family Connections

   Sea urchins belong to a group of animals called echinoderms (ih-KEYE-nuh-durms). Echinoderms vary greatly. But, they all have tube feet.

   There are about 6,000 echinoderm **species**. Other echinoderms include sand dollars, starfish, sea cucumbers, brittle stars, and feather stars.

Sand dollars are round, flat creatures that resemble coins. When they are living, they are covered in brown spines. But when they die, their test turns white.

Brittle stars look like starfish. But, the round shape of a brittle star's center is more apparent than a starfish's center.

Feather stars attach their bodies to the ocean floor. Then, they let their frilly arms sway in the water. This is how they catch tiny organisms to eat.

Starfish may have anywhere from four to 50 arms. The smallest starfish are under one-half inch (1 cm) wide. Other starfish grow to as large as 40 inches (102 cm) across!

There are about 500 sea cucumber species. Some can grow to be 24 to 36 inches (61 to 91 cm) long. A sea cucumber can throw out some of its inside organs. This can confuse predators and help it stay safe. Later, the body parts grow back.

Dinnertime

Sea urchins mostly eat plants such as **kelp** and **algae**. But, some also eat live animals. These include sea sponges, brittle stars, and **mollusks**. Sometimes, even dead animals become sea urchin food.

Sometimes too many sea urchins gather in one area. If this happens, a kelp bed may be eaten and destroyed by the hungry sea urchins.

A World Of Danger

For some animals, sea urchins are a favorite meal. Sea otters eat purple sea urchins that live off the U.S. West Coast. And, sea urchins are an important food source for wolf eels.

Atlantic wolffish do not seem bothered by the sea urchin's sharp spines.

Many sea urchins have **venom** to help protect them from predators. Some have venom in their spines. Others have special **organs** that deliver venom. These organs are usually shorter than the spines.

Fascinating Facts

❋ Some ancient Egyptians used pencil urchin spines to write on slate tablets.

Pencil urchin

* Some sea urchins use their spines to help them hide from predators. They use their spines to toss **algae** and shell pieces on top of their bodies.

* The fire urchin has very short spines. But each spine is tipped with a **venom** sac. So, it can defend itself against many larger creatures.

Coleman's shrimp are not harmed by fire urchin venom. So, they sit among its spines for protection.

Learn And Explore

In 1875, biologist Oskar Hertwig was the first person to witness an egg being **fertilized**. It happened when he was studying a sea urchin. Since then, sea urchins have been important to scientists studying animal reproduction.

Scientists hope to learn more about human reproduction from sea urchin studies.

IMPORTANT WORDS

alga a plant or plantlike organism that lives mainly in the water.

fertilize to make fertile. Something that is fertile is capable of growing or developing.

kelp a large, brown seaweed.

mollusk an animal with a soft, unsegmented body without a backbone. Snails, clams, and squid are all mollusks.

organ a part of an animal or a plant that is composed of several kinds of tissues and performs a specific function. The heart, liver, gallbladder, and intestines are organs of an animal.

plankton small animals and plants that float in a body of water.

species living things that are very much alike.

suction to draw out using force.

venom a poison produced by some animals and insects. It usually enters a victim through a bite or a sting.

WEB SITES

To learn more about sea urchins, visit ABDO Publishing Company on the World Wide Web. Web sites about sea urchins are featured on our Book Links page. These links are routinely monitored and updated to provide the most current information available.

www.abdopublishing.com

INDEX